LIVE YOUR BEST LIFE

Taking Charge and Organizing Your Life

CRISTINA ABATE

Copyright © 2014 Cristina Abate

All rights reserved.

ISBN-10: 1533060843
ISBN-13: 978-1533060846

This information is protected by intellectual property laws, including trademark and copyright laws. Except as permitted under the Act (for example a fair dealing for the purposes of study, research, criticism, review or personal use) no part of this book may be reproduced or transmitted in any form or by any means, electronic or mechanical, including photocopying, recording, or by any information storage and retrieval system, without written permission from the author. Every effort has been made to trace and acknowledge copyright. The author apologies for any accidental infringement and welcomes information to redress the situation.

Disclaimer

The information is of a general nature and does not take into account your personal situation. The information presented is for educational purposes only. The author will not bear any responsibility or liability for any action taken by any person, persons or organization on the purported basis of the information contained in this book and any supporting material. References to other information, websites or events should not be understood as an endorsement of such information, website or events. Every effort has been made to ensure that this book is free from errors or omissions. However, the author shall not accept responsibility for injury, loss or damage occasioned to any person acting or refraining from action as a result of material in this book whether or not such injury, loss or damage is in any way due to any negligent act or omission, breach of duty or default on the part of the author.

CONTENTS

Introduction 0

Self Analysis: Getting To Know You 1

Thinking About What Needs To Change 5

Relationships 6

Self Confidence and Empowerment 8

Getting Organized 13

Goal Setting 23

Plan To Achieve 27

Evaluation 29

Conclusion 31

INTRODUCTION

I want to thank you and congratulate you for buying this book, "**Live Your Best Life**".

Moving forward is a simple thing. Or is it?

In a modern world where we are pressured to outperform the next person, earn more money than we did yesterday, do better this time next year, it seems like a never-ending climb to fulfillment.

This guide encourages you to seek what you wish to find, then hopefully achieve, but undergoing a "get to know you". It encourages you to review where you currently sit, then where you'd like to be. It encourages you to think carefully about what you want.

In discovering what you might like to change, this guide gives you tips on how to achieve change, providing you with practical advice on how to introduce change, and then continue along this path to achieve the ultimate change that you are looking for.

Many of us have heard that the final result is not important, it is the lessons that we learn along the way. This is true, as life is a collection of days to experience and learn from, that culminate eventually to an end point. Should we have to wait until this end point to be happy? I don't think so. Learning, loving and experiencing along the way is truly living. This guide encourages us to live each day, with an end point in mind. Getting there should be part of the fun.

Some are risk averse, choosing to live quiet, uneventful lives, living day by day, simply and basically. Others are risk takers, wanting to squeeze the most out of life each and every day, participating in adventurous and exhilarating activities often, being active and social, having a wide and diverse friendship circle, and being involved and doing almost everything that they can.

Most of us wish for a life somewhere between these two extremes. Whichever life we choose or desire, we should live it, do it wholeheartedly, focusing our energy into living each day fully to the beat of our own drum so to speak. We are all individual. We are all different. We are all capable of living the lives that we choose for ourselves. Our task is deciding what is right for us, which direction to take, then make plans and take action to achieve this.

This is a short guide providing useful information on how to achieve this. It will lead you through a series of steps, categorized into four main areas.

This guide can be used as a practical motivational tool, providing you with valuable advice on how to achieve your goals.

The quotes that I have included in this book are inspirational to me and quotes that I have collected over time, hence I haven't provided their source, only the author. I keep these inspirational quotes, along with pictures and images that inspire me at my desk where I sit to do my work each day.

Thanks again for purchasing this book, I hope you enjoy it!

SELF ANALYSIS: GETTING TO KNOW YOU

Getting to know you is often the hardest part.

Most of us have a general idea of what we do and don't like, however to pinpoint a specific direction that we wish our lives to take is difficult.

I believe this to be because we think this is our one and only chance to do something with our lives. However, this is untrue.

Our lives are constantly changing as we grow and have different influences and people come into and then out of our lives.

Each stage of our lives offers a myriad of experiences adding to a rich and wondrous life, however we often don't rejoice in the wonder of our lives, often we feel frustrated that perhaps we are not doing what we ought to be doing.

The way that we interpret our lives, its progress, its successes, and its pitfalls are usually our own interpretation. Life events serve to teach us something - whether that teaching be a new skill, a moment of appreciation for what we have, or a lesson that it is the wrong thing to be doing, all of what we gain can be seen as positive, shedding light on how we view ourselves

Happiness too is an interpretation. Often I have felt happy one moment, and completely miserable the next. Happiness is not permanent. It is a feeling - one that passes and changes, depending on our influences at the time, our level of satisfaction at that moment.

If we strive to satisfied most of the time, then overall we can achieve a happy life. Deciding what will make yours a happy life, or a satisfying one requires thought, then a plan.

We often feel pressured by the confines of our limited resources, and on how best to use them. Whether these resources are financial, educational, professional, or human (as in relationships) we need to work with what we have, be grateful for what we have, and build on them.

We have ingredients within us from which to build successful lives - examples of such ingredients are intelligence, determination, capacity for hard work, curiosity, compassion, ability to learn, physical strength, artistic ability, to name a few. Ingredients work synergistically to create a magnificent whole. Different combinations of ingredients make us individuals, each of us being unique and magnificent human beings.

To determine what our unique ingredients are, do the following:

Look at specific experiences that occur in your daily life and list what you do well, what could do better, what you would like to do better.

Which individual traits shine?

Which traits would you like to hide?

Which traits would you like to see yourself develop?

When do you feel at your best?

Who brings out your best?

When have you felt the happiest so far?

What were you doing at this time and who with?

What makes you anxious?

What situations do you avoid?

What do you imagine yourself doing?

What would you imagine yourself doing, if you could imagine anything?

How would you feel if you were doing what you imagine yourself doing?

LIVE YOUR BEST LIFE

Is this how you feel now?

How badly do you want to feel this way?

Note the answers to each of the above questions, over several days.

Can you see a pattern emerging?

Are the answers the same from day to day thereby indicating a trend?

If the answers are different each day, then you need to think harder, being honest, ensuring that you are thinking deeply enough about your real self.

Take your time. In undergoing this activity, you should see a trend emerging in your answers, a profile developing. Undergoing this process will uncover and reveal a blueprint for who you are, and identify what you hope to achieve. It serves as a starting point to develop a plan.

Ultimately, we are responsible for the lives that we choose to live.

Some of us are not so lucky to be able to make these choices for themselves, being born into circumstances that we did not create. However, many of us are able to make choices to change the path of our lives.

The great Katherine Hepburn is known to have said, "Well, as one goes through life one learns that if you don't paddle your own canoe, you don't move." This is illustrative of the fact that we need to take control of our lives, discover what we want from our lives, and create our environment.

Many have overcome desperate situations to build rewarding, worthwhile lives, in the midst of the most terrible circumstances. We hear of Holocaust survivors, who have lost so much, endured much pain, however chosen to make the most of their lives by seeking opportunities for growth, love and fulfillment. Others have offered inspiration to others, doing extraordinary things with their lives, achieving insurmountable tasks, mostly through commitment to determination to succeed, and having a clear vision on how they wish to live.

Three inspiring stories follow however there are thousands that we could point to - perhaps you can find your own story?

Sir Edmund Hilary and Sherpa Tenzing Norgay were the first men to climb Mount Everest in 1953. Together they overcame physical and psychological near impossibilities to achieve this feat, in the most treacherous and dangerous of conditions. This achievement, given its monumental, ground-breaking and world famous proportions is coupled with a lesser known fact - Sir Edmund Hilary devoted much of his life to assisting to build hospitals, schools and facilities for the Sherpa people of Himalaya, thereby contributing enormously to improving their quality of life.

Another remarkable story is that of Helen Keller, becoming deaf and blind at 19 months of age, she lived to be the first deaf blind person to earn a Bachelor of Arts degree. She became famously known as a political activist, advocating for people with disabilities, educator and author, publishing twelve books and many articles.

Mother Teresa, a selfless humanitarian, leaving her family to never seeing or hearing from them again, to educate and serve the poor. She travelled to India, learned several languages to be able to communicate with those that she wished to help, and lived in desperately poor circumstances herself to serve the most impoverished in Calcutta. Her sacrifice is inspirational, driven by kindness, love and generosity for the most lowly in that society, without her not having a hope of survival.

There are many, many more inspirational stories of people overcoming enormous difficulties to achieve wonderful things, and live purposeful, rewarding lives making contributions that have benefitted many. These stories have a common thread - courage, determination and foresight. In everyday, ordinary life we can achieve wonderful things - things that are our personal achievements, our intentions to meet goals we set.

THINKING ABOUT WHAT NEEDS TO CHANGE

Before you set goals, think about how to introduce change into your life. What do you want to change in your life?

What needs to change?

In viewing how to change, go back to the self analysis and remember the traits that were negative, and plan to change these.

Consider what you need to change in order to restore balance to your current situation.

Look at all key areas of your life where improvements can be made:

Emotional
Physical
Financial
Professional
Relationships

Then think about the environments in which these improvements can be made - home, work, community.

Think about the people in your life and how changes can be made to improve these relationships - family, friends, and life partners.
.

RELATIONSHIPS

Audrey Hepburn once said, "The best thing to hold onto in life is each other." Everyone needs to be loved.

In this fast paced, competitive world we sometimes don't make time for the important people in our life, taking for granted that they will always be there.

We tend to want to be with the most interesting, successful and vivacious people, the ones that make us feel and look good.

However, we can't all be interesting, successful and vivacious, and to love and accept ourselves for what and who we are is the first step in nurturing a relationship.

How you feel about yourself, what influences you & affects you, will ultimately influence the health of your relationships.

Determine what you need to maintain your emotional health, before you can look to improve your relationships.

Ultimately, once you've decided what you need and want from a relationship, you are in a better position to ask for it.

Make friends with yourself - accept yourself for who you are and what you stand for. You are unique. You are an individual. Celebrate this.

Think about those people who drain energy from you, make you feel inadequate, make you feel self-conscious and un-worthy of their company. These are people that you can probably do without.

If they want a meaningful relationship with you then they should not be making you feel inferior, inadequate.

Perhaps they are the problem. If you can walk away from them then do so, however, sometimes these people may be within our families, our workplaces, in which case we will have no choice but to manage these types of relationship. Work out a way to deal with them on our terms.

Having self confidence, believing in yourself, and believing that you matter are major steps forward in dealing with difficult relationships. Stand up for what you believe. Eleanor Roosevelt said, "No one can make you feel inferior without your consent."

SELF CONFIDENCE AND EMPOWERMENT

Psychological preparation is important to achieve goals set.

Lacking self confidence and feeling disempowered are factors that will prevent you from moving forward.

- There are many ways to improve self confidence including:
- Recognizing what you do well and do more of these
- Acknowledge what you have achieved and
- Thinking positively about yourself, avoiding the negative self-talk.

Building self esteem is developed when we continue to challenge ourselves, striving to reach higher limits giving us a sense of achievement and accomplishment. Goal setting helps us to do this.

Focusing attention and effort onto achieving a goal will require one to either use knowledge that they have, past experience and knowledge that they have, or develop additional knowledge or skills to achieve the end point.

In any case, whatever is needed to achieve the goal, any effort put into achieve the goal at all can only be a positive thing for the individual.

Setting goals encourages us to do our best, strive and work harder, and ultimately grow personally, with the ultimate goal of becoming a satisfied, fulfilled and happy individual.

Stepping outside of our comfort zone, experiencing new skills and challenges builds self-esteem. Striving to do better and work harder. Set high standards for yourself, work hard to achieve them, and watch results follow.

You will observe personal growth undergoing this process, and a tremendous boost to self-confidence in trying something new. Doors open when trying new experiences.

You are exposed to new feelings and challenges, revealing aspects about yourself that you may not have known before. Getting to know a hidden side of you can be adventurous and exhilarating, open doors for opportunity.

For example, taking on a new role within the work place that you previously thought yourself unsuitable gives you the opportunity to learn something new and perhaps allow you to get to know your work colleagues better. Applying yourself wholeheartedly to this new challenge may allow embark on new and exciting career change.

Should the experience prove to be a wrong choice, at least you have undergone a learning experience, a transformational change in realizing something new about yourself. This is an example of "nothing ventured, nothing gained", and it is a progressive step in getting to know more about you.

Be open to challenges and invitations to do new things.

Often others may consider that we are suited to a particular role or activity that hadn't occurred to us. This is because others sometimes see us differently to how we see ourselves - seeing aspects of ourselves that we can't see. It is a wonderful thing to be recognized for things that we do well, especially when we don't realize that we have such a natural talent. Follow through on recommendations given to you for new opportunities.

Becoming move involved in your community, school, work environment, or local council can be rewarding as well as connect you with like minded people. Contributing time and skills voluntarily towards a community cause can be a rewarding and enriching experience. It will allow you to meet a new network of people and giving you an opportunity to learn from others and make new friends.

Becoming involved socially is a good way to widen and diversify your circle of friends, exposing you to new opinions and ideas.

Your local council is a good source of activities that are offered within your community, for example walking groups, dancing forums, gardening workshops, book clubs, sporting events and community fairs. Again, becoming involved in activities that you wouldn't normally do, expands horizons and exposes you to new opportunities.

Becoming more involved allows you to discover more about yourself, helping you to realize your strengths, likes, dislikes, also weaknesses. The more that we know about ourselves, the more we can accurately assess what we ought to be doing to lead more fulfilling lives.

Believing in you begins with following four steps:

1) Recognize the things that you can do. The things that you can't do can be worked on or learned. Don't focus on your weaknesses. Positive affirm regularly your strengths, what you can do, and more importantly what you will do. We were all born into the world unable to walk, talk, write, read, count, but the incredible ability to learn, be inspired, think for ourselves. Build on what you know and what you have already learned and accomplished.

2) Stop talking yourself out of things with messages of self doubt. Convincing yourself that you can't accomplish something before you even try is craziness. Train the negative voices inside your head that you can do whatever you put your mind to. Everyone has weaknesses and strengths. Accept what your weaknesses are and be determined to work hard to minimize their impact on your life, or change them into positives. We all have the capacity to change, remodel and improve ourselves if we choose to. Sometimes we are our only limiting factor.

3) Think about what advice you would give yourself if you were an outsider looking in. Often we are good at giving others advice, but lousy at taking our own advice. Draw strength from imagining how others would react, behave in a particular situation that you are struggling with - these others may be your ideal role models, those you know personally, or those you don't know personally, however admire greatly.

4) Put yourself in the picture. Imagine yourself doing what you hope to do. Imagine how you are going to look, feel, behave. Have a very clear vision of what you will achieve.

Feeling empowered, comes with having the self confidence to believe that you can do anything that you put your mind to.

Empowerment allows you to use your own power to gain control of your life, giving yourself permission to live as you believe you should. Empowerment is directly related to well-being.

Well being is influenced by the amount of sleep, exercise, good nutrition, work-life balance and relaxation techniques that we build into our life.

These basic components need to be correctly set in our life in order for feelings of empowerment to have a starting chance. Once the foundation is set, we can build a productive fulfilling life. This is discussed in more detail in "Getting Organized.".

GETTING ORGANIZED

Before stepping into action, we need to prepare. This shouldn't be a lengthy process, just a thorough one. Clearing obstacles from our path, and our mind is a good way to start, preparing the soil to reap a bountiful yield, if you like.

Declutter

Remove from your environment untidiness, congestion and items that serve to get in the way - physically and psychologically.

Waking in the morning should be to clean, inspirational space, not piles of junk and things that serve to remind you how much of a mess you live in. It isn't a good start to the day.

Likewise, is moving to a kitchen that is cluttered with dirty dishes, unpacked food from the night before. Get off to a good start but ending the previous day tidy, packed up and clean.

Cleaning up is much easier if things that are not used often are put away. Perhaps a clean out is necessary, throwing away things no longer used or needed, that are currently serving to block a flow of constructive thought and activity.

If moving through your house is like an obstacle course every day, immediately this is a point of antagonism. If not finding items easily because they are buried beneath clutter, then this causes inefficiency and time wastage.

Meal preparation is easier with a fridge and pantry that is well stocked and organized, and a sink and bench tops that are clean and clear.

Preparing for work each day is made easier with a wardrobe that is well organized and arranged.

Remove items from your life that you don't use and don't need, or haven't used for the last 12 - 24 months. There are many charities that are looking for unwanted, but useful items.

Replace negative patterns of behavior with positive ones

Organizing your physical environment is an important as organizing your emotional, spiritual and psychological environment.

Undergoing a self analysis of your moods, temperament and wellbeing is important to understand triggers for certain patterns of behaviors. Behavioral patterns that you wish to avoid, firstly need to be identified - what sets them off and realizing that you are in a downward spiral of negative behaviors. Only once you have identified this pattern of behavior, you can set upon a counter action to break it.

Changing patterns of behavior with more effective ones requires dedication and perseverance. After recognizing and making yourself aware of the particular behavior that you wish to change, identify the triggers that precede this behavior.

For example, how you feel at the time just prior to engaging in the behavior. If you feel bored, restless, frustrated just prior to a binge eat, recognize these feelings and be aware of them. Next time you feel these, you know that a binge eat is about to emerge, however, if you are aware of this fact, you can prepare and stop your next move.

The next step is to interrupt the behavior that usually follows. Acknowledge that you have recognized the precipitating trigger, and the behavior that follows by vocalizing it. Then continue this interruption by doing something positive, like going for a walk, making an errand, taking a bath - something production, worthwhile but positive, and not detrimental to your wellbeing, or that goes against what you are aiming to achieve.

For example, I have a habit of over organizing - dinner is done, house is clean, Johnny is doing homework, Jenny is practicing piano, lunches for tomorrow have been made, appointments for weekend have been organized but Andrew is not practicing his timetables. Why isn't Andrew practicing times tables? This anomaly in my schedule, the one thing that I am having trouble controlling is irritating me profusely, I'm fixated on this one point that I can't control I can feel my temper rising, I begin to nag him and it becomes a point of tension between us. It becomes a power play between me and Andrew. Andrew has decided to do spelling practice instead. Is this so bad?

In recognizing this pattern of obsessive behavior that I don't like about myself, I decide to do something different to break the pattern of behavior. I go for a walk. I return home refreshed, calm having had the opportunity to de-stress.

My over obsessing about having to control everything is something that I don't like about myself, and it serves only to annoy all those around me. It becomes counterproductive. Knowing this, I have decided to embark on a strategy to change this behavior, a strategy that will break the negative pattern of behavior and replace it with a positive one.

Changing behavior that is ingrained is a process that will not happen overnight. Behaviors that have been repeated hundreds of times throughout our life have been deeply reinforced through repetition.

Change requires motivation in order to change. If you are motivated, and determined that you want to change then you need to make a conscious effort to perform the correct behavior, over and over, until you are no longer doing it consciously - until it becomes an ingrained behavior.

Be mindful – meditate

The benefits of meditation are well documented. There are many types and techniques, suffice to say that the method most effective for you needs to be determined by you.

Daily meditation is essential for calming the mind, regaining focus, and coming to terms with how you feel at the moment, adding clarity to current thought processes and restoring mental agility.

Finding thirty tranquil minutes per day to live in the moment, be complete present is empowering, rejuvenating and restorative. It brings harmony into your life and makes you feel happy.

Its benefits are physical as well as mental, reducing stress, lowering hypertension, improving sleep, reducing anxiety.

The myriad of benefits to practicing meditation daily are numerous, so much so that meditation should be an essential part of the daily routine.

The importance of basic routine

Every day, routine tasks are mundane, repetitive and mostly boring.

We feel that there are many more interesting, and productive ways that we could be spending our time. However, rather than feel miserable and resentful about having to do them, and since they consume a significant part of our day, we might as well find some way to enjoy doing them.

Remind yourself how wonderful you will feel once the job is done, how clean the house will look, how wonderful it will be that the fridge and pantry are stocked, how terrific it will feel to have the washing done, folded, ironed and put away. Focus on the reward of the feeling satisfied at the end of it.

Having a daily routine is important for building structure into you day, setting time aside work, exercise, meal times, mundane chores and time for enjoyment.

Organize your week, setting time aside for getting jobs done, with the promise of fitting time for you too.

As each day begins, scan your diary to ensure that you are aware of forgotten commitments. Then have a clear vision of your day, what you will be doing, and most importantly, how mentally you will approach the day - with a positive or negative attitude.

Getting organized also means recognizing those mundane activities that need to be done, and do them so that they have less impact on your life.

For example, don't let that pile of ironing become so high that it becomes burdensome - instead, put fifteen minutes per day to attend to ironing, or forty-five minutes every third day.

Similarly, meal preparation is much easier if you are well prepared. Plan meals for the week ahead and shop accordingly for an hour on the weekend. This way, time is not wasted shopping for ingredients after work, when you are tired and stressed. You could be attending a yoga class instead, for example, or doing something to unwind from your working day.

Cluster mundane tasks and activities, for example, grocery shopping, running errands, picking up dry-cleaning could be done with the same time frame, same trip.

Changing your view towards having to do these repetitive and boring tasks is also important. View doing them as important to sustain life and a good standard of living, and not doing them means disorganization, an unfed family, unclean clothes, homework not done, which causes far more upset than doing the chores.

Bring mindfulness into doing the chores - being present in the moment makes walking the dog more enjoyable, allowing you an opportunity to unwind while you spend time with your beloved pet.

Finding enjoyment in everything that you do, makes each moment, even those spent doing chores, precious.

Structure and routine is important to create a basic, functioning life: get up in the morning at a reasonable time, wash your face and brush your teeth, shower, dressing, prepare a nutritious breakfast, tidy up - all of this prepares you to begin the day.

Maintaining a strict, basic routine daily, allows you then to build on it, for example, adding other activities that improve the quality of your life, such as work, study, exercise, meditation and reflection, time for family and friends and entertainment.

Following a daily routine creates a life that is purposeful. However, don't over commitment as overloading your schedule can cause you to feel overwhelmed, unable to achieve everything you had hoped. Develop a routine that is flexible, with spare time for impromptu changes leads to a more content life.

You are the most important person in your life. Without you, the wonderful things that you do, for example, looking after family and loved ones, cannot occur.

Many of us are constantly giving to others without giving much to ourselves. Particularly those of us looking after young children, where our efforts cannot be appreciated for many years to come, make us exhausted. Continuing to do this to ourselves will eventually lead to us not being able to care optimally for others.

Avoid "burn out" by doing things that you enjoy as often as you can, and ensuring that you obtain sufficient exercise and rest. Simple things like taking the time to sit down to have a cup of tea can be enormously restorative. So is having coffee with a friend, seeing a movie or show, reading a book, visiting an art gallery or museum, going for a walk - whatever your heart desires.

Personal presentation, display of good manners and positive self image are important factors that will a role in deciding how you successful you will be.

Careful attention to personal hygiene and grooming is mandatory and expected. The attitude that you display is paramount in convincing someone that you are keen and serious about achieving your goal.

People will be impressed and interested in helping you if you have the correct attitude - an attitude that shows determination to succeed, willingness to learn, and exudes self respect and confidence.

How you make someone feel is often more important than what you say.

Often your body language will say for you what you really mean, and the saying that people make their mind up about you within the first fifteen seconds of meeting you is often true.

Using good eye contact, and clear speech and communication, with a smile and handshake demonstrates confidence and authority that you are knowledgeable of what you want.

Finally, self belief that you have the ability to achieve your goal is essential. You must convince yourself that you can do it, that you will acquire the skills and knowledge to succeed. Only once you believe this and confidently work towards achieving it, will you be able to convince others.

The importance of gratitude

While our circumstances may not be perfect, there is gratitude to be felt for small miracles that occur each day. There is always something positive we can learn or take away from a seemingly bad situation - the friendships we make, the knowledge we gain or the comfort we receive.

Remember to live in the moment. Enjoy this moment as if it will not occur again.

Life is a journey made up of a collection of moments - we must focus on enjoying each one.

In achieving goals, it is important what we learn along the way, acknowledging and enjoying each reward, each inch of progress.

I particularly like this passage, written by Sir William Ostler, that I came across some time ago, as it clearly illustrates how important "now" is:

"There are two days in the week about this I never worry. One of these days is yesterday with its cares and frets and pains and aches. All its mistakes and blunders have passed forever beyond my control. It was mine. It is God's. The other day that I do not worry about is tomorrow - tomorrow with its possible adversities, burdens, perils. Its large promise and performance, its potential failures and mistakes is far beyond my mastery as is its dead sister yesterday. Tomorrow is God's day. It will be mine. There is left then for myself one day in the week - today. Any person can fight the battles of today...It is only when we add the burdens of those two awful eternities, yesterday and tomorrow, such burdens as only Almighty God can sustain, that we break down. It isn't the experience of today that drives people mad; it's the remorse for what happened yesterday and the fear of what tomorrow might bring. Those are God's days, leave them to Him."

Reflection

Reflecting is a useful way of working through a situation. Rather than turning events over and over in your head to find a solution, write the events down to try to make sense of the situation.

Following a process for reflecting will help you to look at a situation that is constantly on your mind in a systematic way.

Firstly, write down the sequence of events - what happened and how it left you feeling. Be brief and succinct, but factual and honest.

Secondly, give you view point on how you believe it should have been resolved.

Thirdly, write done how you will react or deal with the situation if it happens again - or in other words, what you've learnt from the experience.

Reflection is an effective way of moving forward, by organizing your thoughts and coming to terms with what has happened. It forces you to actively think about something that has happened that you can't let go of, and try to make sense of it.

Often through the process of reflection, you come to see things differently, from a different angle, discovering more about yourself that you didn't know before. Reflection is a process allowing you to let go, and move on.

Spending time in solitude is also a good time to reflect and just be.

Whether this is at home, going for a walk, spending time alone with nature, precious "me" time is rejuvenating, leading to having a sense of self-awareness.

Solitude provides an opportunity for you to be content in your own company. It is not a state loneliness, feeling alone or yearning for company. It is a time for little things sit, letting the dust settle, in our busy lives where we often feel that we are running around in circles not achieving anything, usually because we feel overwhelmed by all that is going on.

Solitude is restorative, helps us to re act and rejuvenate, preparing us to return to our normal, everyday lives with clear, uncluttered mind.

Work - our livelihood

Work is a part of our life.

Whether it is paid work, work within the home or work within the community, it is our contribution to society.

Working can provide us with a sense of pride and achievement, allowing us to feel personal satisfaction.

In the words of Madam C J Walker, "There is no royal, flower-strewn path to success. And if there is, I have not found it, for if I have accomplished anything in life it is because I have been willing to work hard."

Working in an environment where we are doing what love to do is an ideal for many of us. However few actually achieve this ideal. This is usually because we are fearful of taking risks and moving outside of our comfort zone. If we are in a secure, comfortable job, we are reluctant to give it up although we may be unhappy with what we are currently doing.

Goal setting can assist change within the work environment. It helps you to focus your efforts towards achieving an end result, undergoing personal development and growth along the way.

Sometimes you need to do more than just think about what you would like to do, you need to do. Actually try it, see if it's for you. For example, begin "doing" in your spare time. Ask someone that you know doing what you think you would like to do, if they wouldn't mind you spending time with them observing, helping them out so that you may be able to get an idea if you like doing what they do, or if you have the ability to learn the new skill. This is a safe way to try, while having the safety net of an existing job to fall back on.

If we are able to do everyday what we love doing, work doesn't really seem like work at all. Being able to do this creates an opportunity for us to shine, revealing to the world our true selves as we do the work we love, and feel we were born to do.

Doing more of what you enjoy is the key to becoming more fulfilled each day.

Usually, doing what we enjoy brings a great deal of satisfaction, allowing us to fully embrace our chosen work, and work with enthusiasm.

In doing this it is inevitable that we will deliver a wonderful end result.

Think carefully about what you feel passionately about, what you wish for your life's work to be. Keep that thought as we will come back to it in "Putting pen to paper."

Be inspired - create a pictorial representation of who want to be and what you want

Create an inspirational poster that is reflective of you - displaying your role models, inspirational quotes and stories, images of what you hope to achieve.

The poster serves as a daily reminder of your goals and aspirations, what you hope to become, how you see yourself evolving.

Your poster should be placed in an area where you can see it daily, as a shrine that you adore, a mantra. Make it is personal and meaningful to you. It is your inspirational tool and your constant reminder of where you intend to take your life.

GOAL SETTING

Why is goal setting important?

Plenty of action has already occurred. Preparation is the key step that lays the foundation for goal settings.

Getting to know you, getting organized and developing a routine are key elements that create a basic foundation for moving forward.

Now that they have been carefully thought through, planning and goal setting can begin.

Goal setting assists us to move forward, to focus on where we would like to be and create a plan to achieve it.

Set goals high, therefore you have somewhere to aim your focus in getting there.

Not achieving your goals within a set time frame is not failing to meet that goal, because the progress that you have made so far is further than you would have been had you not set the goal, and not worked hard to achieve it.

Anything that you achieve that is more than yesterday is progress. Progress is continual. Goal setting, focuses your thought processes, and forces you to consider what you want and how to achieve it.

Suddenly, you will be consumed with wanting to achieve your goals, putting time, energy and focuses your attention on achieving them.

Goal setting gives you purpose, motivates you, directs your energy into worthwhile activities. It does this because you now know what you are aiming for, what you want to achieve and then what you need to do to get there. This running around circles type behavior will stop. Once you set goals, you will know why you are doing things, for what end, and you will do them wholeheartedly, with a clear focus and direction.

Setting goals gives you a starting point. The process of goal setting allows you to break down a big goal into achievable targets.

For example, you are a junior employee of a multi-national corporation. Your goal is to become a senior manager of the sales department within ten years. You will achieve this by setting achieving targets, for example, in eighteen months times I will achieve this qualification, head this team and belong to this association, and so on and so forth. Being specific with what you intend to achieve and in what time frame allows you to seek opportunities, take up challenges, learn what you have to learn to achieve your target.

Putting pen to paper

The process of self analysis discussed earlier on required deep thought into what drives you, influences you, and affects you.

You thought carefully about what you enjoy, where your strengths lie, what you can imagine yourself doing if you could do anything you dreamed of.

Carefully refer to this analysis and note the following:

What do I want to achieve?
What don't I want?

These two broad questions can be applied to all, one or some aspects of your life - personal, professional, family, friendships, spiritual, emotional and psychological.

There may be a particular goal that you want to achieve in the workplace, or a business goal; or you may want to completely overhaul your life, making changes in multiple areas.

Goal setting can be used to help you with one area of your life or many areas.

Question one asks you to note down what you want.

Question two asks you to note down what you don't want.

You will find that both of these questions are really one and the same.

Because what you do want will be diametrically opposed to what you don't want, and effectively what you don't want forces to you think about how you can change a dislike into a like and ultimately a goal that you want to achieve.

Be precise. Define exactly what you want to achieve.

Understanding what you want puts you in a position to correctly define your goal, allowing you to be specific about what you want to achieve. We will call this the master or lifetime goal.

The master goal can then be broken down into sub-goals, that is, break the master goal down into smaller goals, each with different time frames, and each being a specific task that contributes to the master goal.

Ensure that your sub-goals are achievable targets. They can be incremental, the first sub- goal needed to occur first, thereby contributing to the success of the second sub-goal, and so on, until the master goal is achieved.

Once you have devised your master goals, and then broken down the master goal into manageable, achievable sub-goals, understand how you will have measured the success of each sub-goal, knowing when it is achieved allowing you to move onto the next sub-goal.

Prioritize sub-goals so that they can be achieved in an order that makes sense, and perhaps contributing to the success of the next goal.

It is vital that when setting your goals, you ensure that they are meaningful to you, and are not someone else's goals.

Don't set goals that are going to please your mother, your wife, and or your children.

Set goals for yourself, that you want to achieve for your happiness and fulfillment.

Only then will you be living your life as you see it and want it to be, ultimately becoming fulfilled and satisfied.

Ensure that your goals can be measured, for example in quantifiable terms, or when a particular event has occurred within a defined time frame, thereby allowing to you to observe if you are on track.

Your goals should be structured so that achieving them is determined entirely by you, not by the circumstances of your environment.

For example, you should not aim to climb to the top of the corporate ladder within the company that you work in if you have knowledge that the company is soon to be dissolved. This is an event beyond your control, and will surely prevent you from achieving your goal.

PLAN TO ACHIEVE

We all have the ability to think, to learn, to grow.

Most of us have at least a basic understanding of literacy and numeracy that can be built upon.

Some of us have natural talents and abilities such as artistic skill, or physical flair, which can be refined and developed further.

Everyone has a different starting point, and combined with the skills that we have, our preparedness to learn and a determination to succeed, we all have the ability to achieve our end point.

Develop a plan to bring your idea, vision to life.

Find out what you need to do to achieve your goal. Enquire about the resources that are available to you, for example, the correct people to ask for guidance, the financial capital that you might need the specific skills and qualifications that need to be attained.

Don't become overwhelmed with a lack of knowledge, lack of experience that you have because with the correct motivation and determination as these can be gained. Having no knowledge or experience just means that you have harder to work, and this is not an insurmountable feat.

The old saying, "where there's a will there's a way" is true - if you are determined to do something, you will find a way to do it, even if it seems impossible.

Make the commitment that you will change

It is all well and good to set goals, and plan to change, however without making a firm commitment to yourself that you will change, goal setting is ineffective.

Albert Einstein said, "If you do what you always did, you will get what you always got." If you want to change, you can - however, action is required from you, and only you.

Everyone has the capacity to initiate change.

Believing that you can do it, that you have set goals that are achievable is also a key, essential point.

Henry Ford said, "Whether you think you can or think you can't you're right." At the end of the day you will decide what you will do and where to direct your energy within your life.

Making changes can be done across all areas and across different time frames. Decide upon what you would like to change on a daily, weekly, monthly, and yearly basis.

For example, each day I will begin with stretching exercises for five minutes before I shower. Each year, I will visit a foreign place, join a volunteer group or learn a new skill.

EVALUATION

Soon you'll be able to tell if things are working out.

If things are not going as you had expected, look for solutions.

Learn from what you've done.

Perhaps this is an opportunity to re-examine your goals.

Check that your goals reflect your true passion, your desired direction. Don't be deterred.

I once heard an interview by a self- made millionaire who said that most people fail three times, before they finally succeed.

Go through the goal setting process again, to set new sub goals or make adjustments to existing ones. You may need to widen or shorten time frames set for sub-goals; perhaps you've chosen time frames that are unachievable.

If you haven't achieved your goal exactly as you imagined it, you will have gained some positive benefit, or grown personally along the one.

Examine what you have achieved, and use this as inspiration to continue on your journey.

A happy and fulfilled life comes with continual growth and development, often as a result of concentrating effort and attention towards achieving a goal.

Chart your success using a diary or calendar.

Allow yourself to adjust plans as you go along - perhaps there were unforeseen factors that you hadn't thought of that they now come into play. Adjustments should not change the big picture and may be necessary to achieve your ultimate goal.

Ultimately we want to see continuous progress - even small achievements contribute to the overall picture in some way.

As one drop of water begins to fill a glass, it combines with many to fill a jug. Even setbacks, whilst seeming negative at the time, help us to reconsider various important changes that may be necessary along the way, all for a better outcome.

Directing our attention and effort towards achieving a well thought of goal, rather than a non-goal activity, will result in a positive outcome, whether that be personal growth, recognition of extra effort exerted within a work situation, or seeing a positive change in a personal relationship.

Focusing on achieving your goal requires a commitment to be made that effort will be exerted to achieve the goal.

Feelings of success and achievement have a positive impact on happiness and well-being, making this alone a reason to set goals and strive to achieve them.

CONCLUSION

Thank you again for purchasing this book!

I hope this book was able to help you live your best life.

I appreciate you for taking the time out of your day or evening to read this book, and if you have an extra second, I would love to hear what you think about this book by leaving a review on Amazon. I would greatly appreciate it!

Go to http://amzn.to/16CTd6N

If the links do not work, for whatever reason, you can simply search for the title "Live Your Best Life" on the Amazon website.

Thank you again, and I wish you nothing but the best!

Cristina Abate

HERE IS A BOOK I RECOMMEND CALLED "FOLLOW YOUR OWN PATH"

This is the coolest book I have ever read and by purchasing a copy you put another copy into the hands of someone less fortunate as the author's mission which is to inspire people to do what they love that also contributes to humanity. That is a win/win/win.

Who Is This Book For?

This book is for anyone who is hungry.

Anyone who wants more out of life.

Anyone who knows that they have more to give, share and experience.

Anyone who feels deep down, in their heart, that they are here for a reason.

It's a book for people who feel stuck, lost, depressed or even suicidal.

In particular, it's for, entrepreneurs who are struggling, school leavers who are lost, employees who are bored or in a job they hate and redundees who feel discarded.

Today, more than ever in history, people need more direction and less information.

This book will put you on the right path, YOUR PATH.

Who Is This Book NOT For?

You should not get this book until you are certain that you truly wish to change your life and you are 100 percent committed to it.

Ask yourself these 2 questions:

1. Do I want to make a change voluntarily, completely of my own choice?
2. Do I really want to change my life?

If you cannot honestly say "Yes" without hesitation to both questions, then it is better that you wait until you are serious about changing your life.

As one monk famously said "We want only warriors… victims need not apply".

Go to: http://amzn.to/2kQC9CK

If the links do not work, for whatever reason, you can simply search for the title "Follow Your Own Path" on the Amazon website.

CONTENTS FROM THE BOOK "FOLLOW YOUR OWN PATH"

Who Is This Book For?

Who Is This Book NOT For?

What Is This Book About?

Welcome

Introduction

Who Is Martin Formato?

What Is Success?

3 Simple Steps To True Happiness

STEP 1: FIND YOUR PASSION

Success Mindset

The Beginning And The End

Our Philosophy

You Are A Gift

Believe In Yourself

Which Road To Take

Where Do You Want To Go?

Why Do You Want To Go There?

What Makes You Happy?

You Deserve To Be Happy

What Are Your Superpowers?

What Are Your Values?

Success Formula

What's Your Passion Or Purpose?

Your Personal Vision Statement

STEP 2: DEVELOP YOUR PASSION

Where Are You Now?

Challenges And Obstacles

Re-energize and Inspire

Eliminate Excuses

Your Beliefs

How To Change Your Beliefs

Cognitive Behavioral Approach

Balance Is Important

Comfort Zone Danger

What Resources Do You Have Access To?

Develop Your Passion

Who Are Your Role Models?

Who Is Your Ideal Client?

Who Do You Need To Become?

Morning Ritual

Evening Ritual

Thankful List

STEP 3: GIVE YOUR PASSION TO THE WORLD

Give Your Passion To The World

How Do I Start?

Planning To Live Passionately

10 Reasons Why You MUST Set Goals

Guidelines To Goal Setting

Setting Goals

Time Bound Goals

Prioritize Your Goals

Make Your Goals SMARTER

Your Life Plan On A Page

Milestones

Actions And Tasks

Goal Achievement Plan

Weekly Timetable

Things To Do Today

Living Passionately

14 Reasons Why People Don't Achieve Their Goals

Motivation And Focus

Conclusion

Resources

About The Author

Go to http://amzn.to/2kQC9CK

If the links do not work, for whatever reason, you can simply search for the title "Follow Your Own Path" on the Amazon website.

BONUS: FREE BOOK

Go to the website at www.DoingWorkThatMatters.com and enter your email address to get the FREE book "**Find Your Gift, Passion and Purpose**".

Once you register you will be sent FREE information that will further help you create a life you love.

All you have to do is enter your email address to get instant access.

This information will help you get more out of your life – to be able to reach your goals, have more motivation, be at your best, and live the life you have always dreamed of.

New resources are continually added, which you will be notified of as a subscriber. These will help you live your life to the fullest!

Made in the USA
Monee, IL
28 May 2024